THE PASSOVER TABLE

*New and Traditional Recipes for Your Seders
and the Entire Passover Week*

BY
SUSAN R. FRIEDLAND

PHOTOGRAPHY BY
PENINA

FOOD STYLING BY
EREZ

HarperPerennial
A Division of HarperCollinsPublishers

We would like to thank the following retailers, galleries and individuals, all of whom helped us in many ways to make this book:

Cody's Books; The Jewish Museum of San Francisco; Afikomen; Abrasha; Jan Platt; Thema and David Karasick; The Ginsberg Collection; Fillamento; Britex; Sue Fisher King; Cookin'; Garren Drew of Paul Bauer; The Judah L. Magnes Museum; Diane and Martin Swig; Beryn Hammil; Rabbi Martin Wiener; Cyndie Macdonald of Pavillon Christofle; Antique Traders; John Bright of David M. Brian; Opuzen Design; David Phillips of Mikasa.

For information address:
HarperCollins Publishers, Inc.
10 East 53rd Street
New York, New York 10022

Printed in Hong Kong
A production of David Barich & Associates

Produced by David Barich
Book and Cover Design: Ingalls + Associates
Designers: Thomas Ingalls, Margot
  Scaccabarrozzi
Photography: Penina
Food Stylist: Érez
Assistant: Agnes Halprn
Prop Stylist: Liz Ross

Library of Congress Cataloging-in-Publication Data

Friedland, Susan R.
    The Passover Table: new and traditional recipes for your seders and the entire Passover week / Susan R. Friedland. – 1st. ed.
        p.   cm.
    Includes index.
    ISBN 0-06-095026-9 (pbk.).
    1. Passover cookery.   I. Title.
TX739.2.P37F75   1994
641.5'676437–dc20   93-35991
                                        CIP

97 98 10 9 8 7 6 5 4 3

Let all who are hungry come in and eat, let all who are needy come and make Passover.

–the Haggadah

PREFACE

assover celebrates, primarily, the Jews' Exodus from Egypt. The central meaning of the holiday is liberation, though its focus seems to be food. The Torah instructs Jews that they must experience slavery and redemption as if they themselves were the liberated slaves. To relive the experience, Jews are commanded to observe three rituals: Tell the story of Exodus: "Remember this day, on which you went free from Egypt, the house of bondage, how the Lord freed you from it with a mighty hand …" (Exod. 13:3); to eat matzoth: "At evening you shall eat unleavened bread" (Exod. 12:18); and to refrain from eating or owning *chometz:* leavened bread. "On the very first day, you shall remove leaven from your houses, for whoever eats leavened bread from the first day to the seventh day, that person shall be cut off from Israel" (Exod. 12:15). Matzo is also a reminder of the haste in which the Jews left Egypt, and the Bible instructs: "For seven days thereafter you shall eat unleavened bread … for you departed from the land of Egypt hurriedly—so that you may remember the day of your departure from the land of Egypt as long as you live" (Deut. 16:3).

It is the Torah that defines the holiday and the rabbis who through the centuries have interpreted it. Seven days, for example, is the length of time the Torah specifies, and that is how long Passover is celebrated in Israel. But nineteenth-century rabbis wanted to make sure that all Jews were celebrating at the same time. Diaspora Jews celebrate for an extra day and have an extra Seder to make sure that their celebrations overlap with those in Israel.

Food plays a central role because of the challenge presented by the prohibition against five crucial grains (see page 19). From this Biblical prohibition the rabbis created an elaborate set of rules and regulations of permissible and prohibited foods, which differed from rabbi to rabbi, century to century, and place to place. These customs have been codified into law and account for differences in observance among various groups of Jews. Eastern Europeans (Ashkenazim) had to make do at Passover (and all other times of the year as well), because their inhospitable climate prevented a long growing season or an abundant harvest. Mediterranean (Sephardim) and Middle Eastern Jews had lavish harvests and a large assortment of fruits and vegetables to include in their cooking. The cuisines and traditional foods of the two groups vary widely, though at Passover they and all other Jews observe the same basic restrictions. Most American Jews share an Eastern European heritage, and their foods reflect the holiday dishes served in Vilna and Minsk, Bialystock and Warsaw. The Jews of Istanbul and Aleppo, Algiers and Damascus are fewer in number here and their traditional foods less well known. *Charoset* made with figs or apples, savory matzo "pies" filled with beef or veal, brisket and gefilte fish are all delicious, and Americans should overcome any culinary timidity or xenophobia and try dishes unknown to their ancestors.

This book is for the Jewish cook who at Passover is always searching for new recipes, reliable and tasty, to serve for Seders and for the rest of the holiday. These recipes are kosher if you buy kosher poultry and meats; there is no *trayf* in these pages and there is no *chometz.* So one and all should enjoy a *zeesin Pesach.*

CONTENTS

INTRODUCTION

*I*n *every generation, each individual should feel that he or she personally had gone forth from Egypt, as it is said: "And you shall tell your children on that day saying, this is on account of what the Eternal did for me, when I went forth from Egypt. For the Lord redeemed not only our ancestors; He redeemed us with them."*

This instruction from the Talmud (Pesachim 116b) has been observed by Jews for more than three thousand years. On the fifteenth day of the Hebrew month of Nissan (which corresponds to late March or April), they commemorate in the Seder and the entire week of observance their liberation from two centuries of slavery by the Egyptians.

Passover, or Pesach, literally refers to the "passing over" by God of the homes of the Jews enslaved in Egypt, who were identified by a smear of the blood of a slaughtered paschal lamb on their door posts, when He killed the firstborn son of each Egyptian family. This was the tenth and final plague God visited on the Egyptians and the one that finally persuaded the pharaoh, whose own son lay dead, to free the Jews.

Passover is a continuation and amalgam of earlier holidays: the pagan agricultural one celebrating spring and the first barley harvest, and later the religious holidays of hag ha'Pesach, the festival of the paschal lamb, when nomadic Jewish shepherds offered their spring lambs in ceremonial sacrifice, and hag ha'matzot, the festival of the unleavened bread, when Jews discarded the old bread made from the previous year's flour. Passover also draws its identity from one of the three pilgrimage festivals when Israelites journeyed to Jerusalem to thank God for His bounties and to offer sacrifices at the Temple. It was the only one of the pilgrimage festivals that required women as well as men to travel to Jerusalem. The main Passover service was limited to those who could make the pilgrimage and to those who lived near the Temple ("You are not permitted to slaughter the Passover sacrifice in any of the settlements …" [Deut. 16:5–6]). When the Temple was destroyed, the paschal lamb was eliminated from the Seder, but the other elements of the ritual were transferred to the home, and Seder became a family ceremony with only a symbol of the paschal lamb retained: a roasted shank bone on the Seder plate.

The Talmud emphasizes Passover as the story of continuing deliverance, an event in which all Jews participate. It is meant to ensure that the thread of memory will be unbroken. Each Jew should feel that he himself has fled affliction; she herself must experience slavery and the exhilaration of liberation. This immediacy accounts for the spirit and gusto most Jews bring to the Seder.

The focus for the reliving of the Exodus is the Seder (literally, "order of the ritual"), a ceremonial and didactic meal. The service is presented in the Haggadah (literally, "to tell"), a liturgical text. It retells the story of the Exodus, gives instructions on how to conduct the Seder, explains the Passover symbols, and gives selections from Psalms (113–18), along with songs, riddles, and prayers.

The written Haggadah is more than two thousand years old; before it was transcribed, the head of the family would tell the story of the Exodus, aided by a mnemonic for remembering the order. The formula consists of fourteen words, each of which stands for a specific element of the ritual and is now included, as a chant in rhymed verse, in the introduction to the Haggadah.

Kadesh	blessing over wine
Urhatz	washing hands
Karpas	eating the mild herb
Yahatz	dividing the matzo
Maggid	telling the Passover story
Rahtzah	washing hands
Motzi Matzah	blessing the matzo
Maror	eating the bitter herb
Karekh	the Hillel sandwich
Shulan Orekh	the festive meal
Tzafun	eating the *afikomen*
Barekh	grace after the meal
Hallel	psalms
Nirtzah	conclusion

Haggadahs were improvisatory until the early rabbis adopted the ritual of the Hellenistic symposium for them. Rituals varied and still do: Radical socialist kibbutzim in Palestine didn't mention God; a lesbian Haggadah presents Miriam as the leader, almost ignoring Moses; there is a California Haggadah that has ancient Israelites surfing in the Red Sea; a so-called Liberation Haggadah of the 1960s quoted the "prophet" Eldredge Cleaver. In the 1930s and '40s, Haggadahs were created by Maxwell House and other manufacturers of food products and given away at supermarkets. These free Haggadahs went a long way to codifying the rituals of the Seder. Regardless of the spin or bias of the ritual, it is halachically correct to conduct the Seder in the native language of the participants so that everyone will understand what is going on.

The Haggadah has played an important part in developing Jewish figurative art because it has provided artists with many subjects suitable for illustration: the four sons, the ten plagues, the crossing of the Red Sea. There is a fourteenth-century Spanish Haggadah with pictures of Seder scenes, including a small child asking his father the meaning of the festival. The Amsterdam Haggadah of 1695 was illustrated with copper engravings, made to order for the family of Moses Wesel. A later Amsterdam Haggadah was lavishly illustrated with woodcuts borrowed from a Venetian Haggadah. In modern times, Ben Shahn and Leonard Baskin have illustrated Haggadahs.

Like all Jewish festival meals, the Seder starts with the kiddush—a ritual of domestic worship in which the sanctity of the Sabbath or festival is affirmed over a cup of wine. Because there is such a long service between the kiddush and the actual meal and another long service after the meal, additional cups of wine were added to the Seder. These were incorporated into the ritual as the Four Cups essential to the Seder. They were rationalized as symbols of God's promise of freedom: "I will free you," "I will deliver you," "I will redeem you," and "I will take you" (Exod. 6:6–7). This, however, created a controversy: What about the promise in the next verse of Exodus, "I will bring you into the land"? The Jews had to be delivered to the Promised Land, not just removed from oppression. A fifth cup was added and was filled but not drunk. When the prophet Elijah arrives to announce the coming of the Messiah, he will, according to the rabbis, answer all questions, including whether it is appropriate to drink a fifth cup of wine. This extra cup is named the Cup of Elijah. Many Jews in Israel have added a fifth cup to the last part of the Seder because they feel they are in the promised land.

The Seder follows from the kiddush. The head of the household washes his or her hands (Urhatz) as did the Kohanim (priests) who performed the ritual in the Temple. Then a sprig of parsley is dipped in salt water (parsley, a symbol of spring and hope, is tempered with the salty symbol of tears), a benediction is recited, and everyone eats some mild herb (karpas), usually parsley. The leader breaks off half of the middle matzo and puts it aside to be eaten at the end of the meal—this is the *afikomen* (the word is derived from the Greek and means "after-meal dessert"). Then the poor and the homeless are invited to join in the family Seder. This invitation is in Aramaic, the vernacular of the time, so the poor and uneducated would understand it. It also serves to explain the meaning of matzo: "This is the bread of affliction that our ancestors ate in Egypt. Let all who are hungry come in and eat, let all who are needy come and make Passover."

The central part of the Haggadah (Maggid) consists of introductory and concluding benedictions along with psalms, which were an essential part of the Temple service. The rest of the Haggadah is based on pedagogical principles, because every Jew is duty bound to teach his children about the redemption from slavery—that is the primary objective of the Seder—and much of the liturgy was developed to keep the children alert and interested. The story must be told in depth: "The more one tells about the going out from Egypt the more praiseworthy he is," the Haggadah tells us. Participants are encouraged to interrupt with questions, explanations, interpretations, and insights—this helps to keep the story new and the Seder lively.

The Four Questions (Why is this night different from all other nights? Why on this night do we eat only unleavened bread? Why do we eat only bitter herbs? Why do we dip twice [parsley and bitter herbs]? Why do we all recline?) are traditionally asked by the youngest child at the Seder, though in fact anyone can ask them. The questions were designed as further insurance that the children would be engaged in the ritual. The Socratic nature of these questions and their answers keeps the ritual fresh and enduring. In ancient times the questions were asked after the meal, which makes more sense as the participants had just eaten the matzo and the roast meat of the paschal lamb and had dipped the parsley in the salt water and the bitter herbs in the *haroset*. Originally, there were only three questions; a fourth was added perhaps to match the four sons mentioned in the Haggadah and the four cups of wine. After the destruction of the Temple, the question about the roast meat became obsolete, so a new question was substituted: "Why on all other nights do we eat either sitting or reclined, but on this night we all of us recline?" Leaning on couches at a festive meal was a Roman custom the Jews copied because it emphasized their freedom. The Seder answers three of the four questions, with many digressions. A curiosity of the ritual is that the answer about the paschal lamb relates to a question no longer asked and the question about the leaning posture that replaced it is not answered at all.

The story of the Exodus is told in rabbinical discourses and in a commentary on the Biblical text (Deut. 26: 5–8), concluding with the ten plagues inflicted on the Egyptians along with some speculation about the number and nature of the plagues, raising them from ten to 250. As the plagues are recited, it is customary to remove a drop of wine from the glass for each so that Jewish cups don't overflow because of the Egyptians' suffering. It is here, during the long story of the Exodus, that the four different kinds of sons are discussed: the wise, the wicked, the simple, and the son who asks no questions. There is a *piyut* (prayer-poem) that lists the many favors and benefits that God bestowed on Israel at the time of the Exodus, any one of which would have satisfied the Jews *(dayenu)*.

The Maggid ends with the drinking of the second cup of wine, after the appropriate blessing, followed by a ritual hand washing (Rahtzah). The 2½ matzos are now lifted by the leader and two blessings are said (Motzi Matzah). Pieces of the half of the middle matzo are distributed to be eaten by all the participants. The first blessing thanks God for the bread; the second for "commanding us concerning the eating of matzo."

This is followed by the benediction "concerning the eating of bitter herbs" (Maror). The bitter herb is dipped in the *haroset,* for the second act of dipping. This is another opportunity for the children to question: "Why do we dip twice?" Finally, there is the eating of the three central Passover symbols in one sandwich (Karekh). Matzo, bitter herbs, and *haroset* are combined as a reminder that the sage Hillel, during the time of the Temple, would eat these symbols together, not separately. The rabbis disputed whether they should be eaten together or alone, so we do both.

At last, the festive meal is served (Shulan Orekh). Many Ashkenazim start the meal with hard-boiled eggs dipped in salt water or a soup made of tepid salt water and chopped hard-boiled egg. This may symbolize rebirth and renewal of life, or mourning for the Egyptians who drowned in the Red Sea, or mourning for the Temple. The meal concludes with everyone eating a piece of the *afikomen. Tzafun* in Hebrew means "hidden," and it is the children who search for the halachic dessert, the *afikomen* hidden at the beginning of the Seder and ransomed back to the leader so the Seder can continue. The grace (Barekh) after meals is recited over the third cup of wine. The remaining psalms (Hallel) are now read, and the door is opened as a gesture of welcome to the prophet Elijah. The melodious and gentle *"Eliyahu Hanavi"* is sung. A brief prayer is recited asking God for revenge against the Jews' enemies. This dates from the Middle Ages and was a response to the persecution of the Jews, accused of using the blood of Christian children in their matzos. This portion of the Seder ends with the drinking of the fourth cup of wine.

The formal conclusion of the Seder (Nirtzah, which means "acceptance"), is a request that the prayers were acceptable. Several songs have been incorporated into the last portion of the Seder. The lively melodies and simple verses of *"Ehod Mi Yo'deah"* ("Who Knows One") and *"Chad Gadya"* ("One Kid") were designed to keep the children awake and interested, because by this time the service has gone on well past most peoples' bedtimes. The final chant of the evening is *"l'shanah ha'ba'ah b'Yerushalayim,"* "Next year in Jerusalem."

THE SEDER TABLE

During the Seder the symbolic foods of the holiday are explained and tasted. Representative portions are displayed on a plate placed in front of the leader. The following foods are on most Seder plates:

Karpas: A mild green vegetable such as parsley or celery, or sometimes, onion or potato. At the beginning of the ceremony, the *karpas* is dipped into salt water or vinegar. The *karpas* symbolizes the new growth of spring; the salt water or vinegar represents the tears shed by the enslaved Israelites.

Maror: A bitter herb, usually horseradish among Ashkenazim, and endive, escarole, or romaine lettuce among Sephardim. It symbolizes the intense bitterness of slavery.

Charoset: A sweet spread made from fruit, nuts, and wine, it represents the mortar the slaves prepared for the building of the pharaohs' cities and pyramids.

Zeroah: A roasted shank bone (or sometimes a roasted poultry neck), which represents the paschal lamb that was always sacrificed at the Temple before the Pesach festival and then roasted for the meal. Some think the shank refers to God's outstretched arm (*zeroah*, in Hebrew) as He delivered the Jews from bondage. Because the Jewish sacrificial system was abandoned after the destruction of the Second Temple, some contemporary Jews never eat lamb; others eat it specifically to remember the paschal sacrifice. Because the laws of *kashrut* forbid the consumption of the sciatic nerve, kosher-keepers do not eat legs of lamb for fear of getting a rear rather than a foreleg. Many Israelis find this Diaspora custom unfathomable; they claim to have a method of removing the sciatic nerve, thereby making all parts of the lamb acceptable. Some vegetarians substitute a freshly roasted mushroom or a roasted beet.

Baytzah: A roasted egg. This is another symbol of a supplemental festival offering always brought to the Temple on Pesach. The egg also symbolizes the mourning Jews still feel for the loss of the Temple. Vegans substitute a potato or the pit of an avocado.

The Seder plate—*k'arah*—always follows this organization:

baytzah		*zeroah*
	maror	
karpas		*charoset*

Other items on the Seder table are three matzos placed together on a plate, folded in one or two large napkins or in a special matzo cover. The three are necessary because two loaves are required for every festival and Sabbath; the third is needed to break in half for the *afikomen.* The three matzos are also invested with symbolic meaning: the three religious divisions of the early House of Israel—Kohan, Levite, and Israelite—and the forefathers Abraham, Isaac, and Jacob. There should be enough matzos for each diner to have at least half a piece. All the matzos should be covered during the Seder, which is the only time Jews are obliged to eat matzo; the rest of the week it is optional.

Small bowls of salt water should be placed around the table for dipping. Each diner should have a wineglass, and there should be a cup for Elijah. Calculate four or five cups (each holding between three and five ounces) of wine per person. And the wine should be marked "kosher for Passover," though it does not necessarily have to be sweet. A pillow or cushion should be placed on the left arm of the leader's chair to symbolize the reclining of all the participants.

RECIPES FOR THE SEDER PLATE

Ashkenazik Charoset

Symbolic of the mortar and bricks that the enslaved Jews used to build the pharoahs' cities, this sweet food is delicious. Make enough so people can eat it with the meal—it's that good.

> **1 pound apples**
> **1¼ cups walnut halves**
> **¾ tablespoon ground cinnamon**
> **3 to 5 tablespoons sweet wine**

1. Peel, core, and chop the apples. Add the walnuts and chop finely.

2. Add the cinnamon and wine and mix well. The *charoset* should have the texture of a coarse paste. Taste and add more cinnamon or wine.

Makes 4 cups

Sephardic Haroset

> **1 cup pitted dates (about ½ pound)**
> **½ cup raisins**
> **1 apple**
> **½ cup walnut pieces**
> **1 teaspoon grated fresh ginger**
> **¼ cup sweet wine**

Combine all the ingredients except the wine in a wooden bowl and chop finely with a *mezzaluna*. Stir in the wine to make a coarse paste.

Alternatively, put all the ingredients in a food processor and pulse a few times.

Makes 2 cups

Baytzah

To roast the egg: Place the egg in cold water, bring to a boil, reduce heat, and simmer for about 12 minutes. Place the boiled egg in a preheated 400°F degree oven for 20 minutes, until it is brown and cracked.

Zeroah

To roast the shank bone: Place it in the oven with the egg. It will take between 40 and 60 minutes to brown.

THE PASSOVER PANTRY

The basic principle of Passover observance is that "Seven days you shall eat unleavened bread" (Exod. 12:15). "Seven days shall there be no leavened products found in your homes, for whoever eats *chometz,* that person shall be cut off from the congregation" (Exod. 12:19).

Chometz is the leavened product that results when any of the five grains—wheat, rye, barley, oats, and spelt—comes in contact with water for more than eighteen minutes, the rabbinic calculation of the time it takes for flour to rise once it is in contact with a liquid. All foods made from these grains are considered *chometz.* Matzo is permitted because it is carefully watched to make sure that the maximum of eighteen minutes is not exceeded. During the post-Talmudic period, some religious authorities prohibited additional foods on Passover because of their similarity to the proscribed grains. In addition to the five major grains, Ashkenazim (Eastern European Jews) by custom do not eat rice, corn, beans, peas, millet, buckwheat, and peanuts or any food made from them. Sephardim (Mediterranean Jews) never instituted the ban on auxiliary foods because their cuisine was dependent on these *kitniyot* (Hebrew for legumes). Sephardic custom differs from place to place. Some people, for instance, permit rice but not beans; others avoid chick-peas because *humus,* their name in Hebrew (and Arabic), sounds too much like *chometz.*

Apart from the forbidden grain-based foods, almost everything is suitable for Passover consumption. The laws of *kashrut* apply, as they do the other fifty-one weeks of the year; strict avoidance of *chometz* and the other forbidden foods is an additional *mitzvah* (religious duty) to keeping a kosher home. The Torah prohibits even owning or deriving benefit from *chometz.* The weeks before the holiday (beginning with Purim, when the eager cook starts her *rossl* [see page 31]), are devoted to a very rigorous spring cleaning. A kind of purification takes place, with particular attention paid to the kitchen and those areas where food is prepared, stored, or eaten.

Packaged food carries a mark (called a *hechsher*) certifying its approval by one or more rabbis for consumption at Passover. It assures the consumer that the manufacturer or purveyor has completely cleaned its facilities and machinery and, of course, has strictly avoided the prohibited foods. More and more foods are deemed kosher for Passover, and the sense of deprivation felt even twenty years ago has largely been eliminated; nowadays, it seems that only bread is forbidden.

Because of the strict prohibition against *chometz,* the eating patterns of observant Jews change during Passover. Though much food is permissible, there is the sense of a different time: The dishes are different, for many traditional foods based on matzos are served only during this short week. Matzo itself, both the symbol of freedom and "the bread of affliction," is a

daily reminder of the Exodus. The holiday is both happy and melancholy, and the rhythm of daily life changes, which is appropriate for a period of time marking so crucial an event in Jewish history.

The items used most are eggs for leavening, chicken fat (see below), and matzo and matzo products. Matzo meal, matzo cake meal, and matzo farfel are all made (under the watchful eyes of at least one rabbi) from whole matzos ground finely or coarsely to resemble those wheat-based foods that are forbidden or whose manufacture is not supervised by at least one rabbi. Potato starch is used as a thickener in place of flour. It is extracted from the potato tuber and ground to a fine white powder.

For rules on kashering your dishes, pots, and homes, consult your rabbi, or *How to Run a Traditional Jewish Household* by Blu Greenberg (New York: Simon and Schuster, 1983), or *The Spice and Spirit of Kosher-Passover Cooking* (written and published by the Lubavitcher Women, 852 Eastern Parkway, Brooklyn, NY 11213).

SCHMALTZ
Chicken Fat

Chicken fat imparts a delicious flavor to foods. It was was accessible to Eastern European Jews, who could not easily find vegetable or olive oil.

6 ounces chicken fat
3 ounces chicken skin, shredded
1 large onion, halved and thinly sliced

1. The largest deposit of chicken fat is in the bird's neck. Remove it from there and from the rear cavity. Save raw fat (well wrapped) in the freezer; it will take the fat from several chickens or a couple of stewing hens to get enough to render. Take the skin from the neck.

2. Place all the ingredients in a heavy skillet and let them cook over medium heat, stirring occasionally, until the fat is reduced to a liquid and the skin and onion are golden and tempting, about 45 minutes.

3. Pour the rendered fat through a sieve lined with cheesecloth into a storage jar. Let it cool before covering tightly and refrigerating for several days or freezing for several months. The *gribenes,* or cracklings, that are left in the sieve are a superb snack, to be eaten right from the sieve; they are also quite delicious in a potato *kugel* or mashed potatoes, though it's hard to keep *gribenes* around long enough to have the opportunity to cook with them.

Makes 1 cup

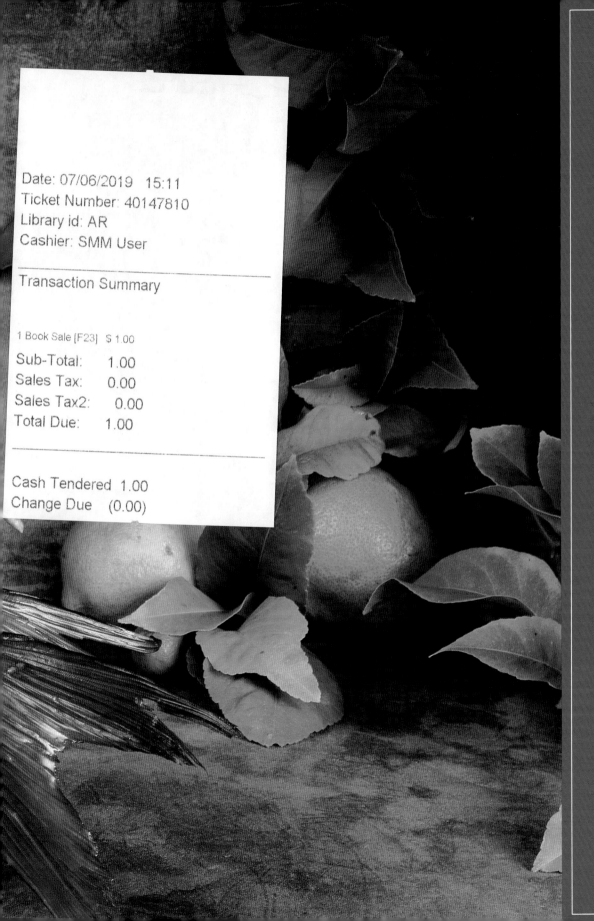

APPETIZERS AND SOUPS

*Seders usually start with chicken soup
served with matzo balls or* mandlen *and
then gefilte fish. These foods are
also good during the rest of the week, and
not only as appetizers: Gefilte fish
makes a really good lunch, as does chicken
soup. The other recipes in this chapter can be
served at Seder and all during the week for
whatever part of the meal you'd like
to eat them. Though the foods are
traditional, don't lock them into whatever
place in the meal your grandmother
would have served them.*

CHICKEN SOUP

All Jewish holidays and many Shabbat dinners start with chicken soup. This rich and delicious version uses stewing hens, if you can find them. Younger chickens will also give you a good soup.

**Two 6- to 8- pound stewing hens, including
neck and giblets but not the liver
5 to 6 quarts water
4 large onions, halved
6 carrots, scraped and cut into large chunks
15 parsley sprigs
10 peppercorns, crushed
Dill
Parsley
Kneidlach (page 26)
Mandlen (page 27)**

1. Remove the fat from the cavities of the hens and set aside for rendering (see page 21).

2. Place one hen in a stockpot with the water and half of the vegetables. The ingredients should barely be covered with water.

3. Bring to a boil and immediately lower the heat.

Skim the foam that rises to the surface and adjust the heat so that only a bubble or two appears on the surface of the liquid. Add the parsley sprigs and peppercorns, partially cover the pot, and simmer for about 2 hours, skimming occasionally. The hen should be tender but not falling apart.

4. Remove the hen to a large platter, and when it is cool enough to handle remove the meat from the bones. Alternatively, let the hen cool in the liquid and then reserve the meat (for the Mina de Pesah on page 48 or a chicken salad) and put the bones and skin back in the simmering soup. Or, let the hen cool in the broth and then proceed. Cook for another hour or so. Strain the soup into a large bowl and discard everything in the strainer. Cool the soup and refrigerate overnight. Remove the fat that has hardened on the surface.

5. For a really superb soup, start again with the just-made defatted chicken stock, the remaining vegetables, the second hen, and more water if necessary to cover the ingredients.

6. Serve with chopped dill, parsley, and *kneidlach* or *mandlen.*

Makes 5 to 6 quarts

KNEIDLACH

Matzo Balls

Matzo balls are relatively simple to make and satisfying to eat. Yet they always generate a great deal of conversation and consultation among the makers and the eaters. Is heavy or light preferred? Small or large? Should seltzer or tap water be used as the liquid?

Matzo balls are mainly about texture, and most people do prefer light to heavy. The one thing that gives them flavor is chicken fat, and the one thing that ensures a good texture is refrigerating the matzo-ball mixture for several hours before cooking them. Once you've boiled them, the matzo balls will keep, loosely covered on a platter at room temperature, for several hours.

The best recipe is the one printed on the box of matzo meal, and every brand has the same recipe printed on its side. Here's my recipe, though it's not really mine: It's the one passed down from generation to generation, on the side of the matzo meal box.

4 eggs
½ cup seltzer or water
6 tablespoons schmaltz, melted
Salt
Freshly ground black pepper
1 cup matzo meal

1. Beat the eggs until the whites and yolks are just combined. Stir in the seltzer or water, schmaltz, salt, and pepper. Gradually add the matzo meal, stirring until it is well combined. Cover and refrigerate the batter for at least 1 hour.

2. Bring a stockpot full of water to a boil. Between moistened palms, roll 2 tablespoonfuls of batter into a ball and drop into the boiling water. Repeat until all the batter is used. Cover the pot and cook the matzo balls for 30 minutes. Serve in chicken soup, 1 or 2 to a bowl of soup.

Makes 16 matzo balls

ROSSL

Fermented Beets

These fermented beets are a tradition for Passover. Many Jewish cooks put this up around Purim so that, in time for Passover, they have a supply for hot and cold borscht as well as beet juice for their grated horseradish *(chrain)*.

5 pounds beets
2 quarts water, boiled and cooled to lukewarm

1. Trim, peel, and cube or slice the beets. Place them in a large crock or glass jar with the water, which should cover the beets by about 2 inches. Partially cover the crock with a lid, and cover that with a kitchen towel. Find a convenient but out-of-the-way spot because the *rossl* will be on your counter for about a month.

2. Within a day, a white veil or membrane will rise on the surface. Remove it every other day or so, stir the beets, and cover as before. Continue removing the membrane, making sure the beets are always covered with water—boil and cool additional water if necessary to keep the beets submerged. When the *rossl* is clear and deep red, it is ready to use. Keep refrigerated.

Makes about 1 to 1½ quarts rossl, *plus the beets*

COLD ROSSL BORSCHT

Serve this soup with all the garnishes as a very satisfying lunch, or clear as an appetizer.

For each cup of borscht:
1 cup *rossl* liquid
1 cup slivered *rossl* beets
½ onion
Lemon juice
Sugar
Salt
Freshly ground black pepper

Garnishes
½ cucumber
1 hard-boiled egg
1 tablespoon sour cream or yogurt
1 scallion, chopped
1 small potato, boiled

Put the *rossl* in a saucepan with the slivered beets and the onion. Bring to a boil and simmer for 15 minutes, or until the onion and beets are tender. Remove and discard the onion. Add lemon juice, sugar, salt, and pepper to taste. Unless you have a taste for really tart food, the borscht will take a lot more sugar than you think it can absorb.

Chill before serving with one or more of the garnishes.

CHOPPED LIVER

Because of the length of the Seder and the festive meal and the restrictions on what alcoholic beverages can be served (nothing made from grain), few people serve cocktails before the Seder. However, here's the best Jewish appetizer there is, and it goes nicely with a glass of permissible slivovitz.

1 pound chicken livers
About 5 tablespoons schmaltz
4 cups chopped onions
2 hard-boiled eggs
Salt
Freshly ground black pepper

1. In a heavy skillet over medium heat, cook the chicken livers thoroughly in 1 tablespoon of the schmaltz. Sauté the liver in batches, if necessary, to avoid crowding the pan. (The kosher-keepers' method is to broil the livers under high heat until they are completely cooked. Broiling is the only sure way to remove all the blood from the livers.) Remove to a plate as they are done.

2. Melt 4 tablespoons of the schmaltz in the skillet over low heat and cook the onions slowly until they just start to brown.

3. Put the onions, eggs, and livers through the coarse blade of a meat grinder and then chop with a *mezzaluna* in a wooden bowl—the grandmothers' method. Or, process the livers and onions in a food processor, using a few very short pulses. Be careful, or you will have a liver paste. If you use a processor, chop the eggs by hand and mix them in with a wooden spoon.

4. Taste the liver carefully for salt and pepper—it will need a lot of both. Add more schmaltz if the mixture is too dry. Serve with matzo.

Makes about 3 cups

ENTREES

*The entrees offered here range from
such substantial meat dishes as
pot roast and stuffed breast of veal to quite
light main courses such as matzo meal
pancakes and* matzo brei *that are good
for breakfast, lunch, and dinner. Don't be
locked into convention: Enjoy a* matzo brei
*and salad for dinner; have matzo meal
pancakes for lunch.*
¶ *The recipes that are good for Seders,
large or small, are very forgiving
in terms of timing: They will wait and
wait. See, for example, the tzimmes, the
brisket, the* tagine, *and the stuffed breast
of veal—all can be prepared in
advance and once cooked have a long
grace period before being served.*

POT ROAST

Pot roast is often made from the brisket, which is an alternate name for the dish. Everyone who cooks has a recipe for brisket or pot roast. This very simple one is mine. You can use this method for any sized brisket, first-cut or whole; just remember to cook it with half its weight in sliced onions.

One 7- to 8-pound whole brisket, well trimmed
4 pounds onions, sliced
Salt
Freshly ground black pepper

1. Place the brisket in a pot in which it fits snugly. Add the onions. Cover the pot, place over very low heat or in a 300°F oven, and cook until the brisket is tender, about 3 hours.

2. You can serve the brisket immediately, sliced and surrounded with the onions. Or, put the brisket on a large piece of aluminum foil and wait for it to cool before wrapping and refrigerating it. Strain the onions from the juice and refrigerate them separately. In a few hours or overnight the fat will harden on the top of the cooking liquid. Remove and discard. Puree the defatted cooking juices with the reserved onions. Reheat the the brisket in this very rich gravy, taste for salt and pepper, and serve, thinly sliced against the grain, with the onion gravy.

Serves 10 to 12

STUFFED BREAST OF VEAL

This is a good dish to prepare for a Seder because you can't really overcook it—it waits for the most long-winded Seder leader and the most curious children.

Ask the butcher to trim the breast, make a pocket in it, and crack the large bone to which the ribs are attached to make carving easier.

Stuffing

3 cups chopped onions
¼ cup schmaltz or vegetable oil
1 cup matzo meal
2 tart apples, cored and diced
6 tablespoons chopped parsley
Salt
Freshly ground black pepper
¼ to ½ cup water

One 8- to 10-pound breast of veal
2 cups sliced onions
6 to 12 unpeeled garlic cloves (use more or less, depending on your taste for garlic)
5 to 6 carrots, coarsely chopped

1. Preheat the oven to 350°F.

2. To make the stuffing: Sauté the onions slowly in the schmaltz or vegetable oil until they soften but don't brown. Add the matzo meal, apples, parsley, salt, and pepper. Mix well. Add the water as necessary to bind the stuffing. Let the mixture cool before using. You should have about 4 cups of stuffing.

3. Just before cooking, stuff the pocket of the veal with the stuffing; skewer the opening closed.

4. Scatter the onions, garlic, and carrots in a large roasting pan. Place the roast on top and rub it with salt and pepper. Add enough water to the pan to cover the vegetables but not the veal. Cover the pan with aluminum foil and roast for 2 hours. Remove the cover and cook for an additional hour or so. The top should be crisp and brown.

5. Remove the breast to a cutting board. With a slotted spoon, remove the vegetables to a sieve. Skim as much fat as you can from the cooking liquid. Press the vegetables through the sieve back into the roasting pan. Place over high heat, scraping the pan to loosen the bits stuck to the bottom. Place the sauce in a gravy boat, to pass with the veal.

6. Slice the veal, following the ribs. Each portion should have a bone, stuffing, and some of the crisp top. Calculate 1 rib per serving.

Serves 6 to 8

TZIMMES

A meat and vegetables tzimmes *is* a big deal (see page 70 for a meatless tzimmes and the Yiddish meaning of the word), but it is made in advance and the result is so delicious you forget about the work involved. I cannot imagine Passover without a tzimmes—perhaps that's because we make so much it's eaten for at least five of the eight days. Both this and the vegetable tzimmes are very flexible—if you don't like one of the suggested ingredients, leave it out or make a substitution. It can be reheated again and again and is a wonderful Seder dish.

Vegetable oil
Salt
Freshly ground black pepper
6 pounds lean, meaty flanken (short ribs)
4 cups chopped onions
4 cups boiling water
11 ounces dried apricots
1 pound pitted prunes
3 pounds carrots, scraped and sliced
2 pounds sweet potatoes, peeled and sliced
2 tablespoons lemon juice
1 tablespoon grated lemon peel
1 tablespoon grated fresh ginger
½ teaspoon ground cinnamon

1. Film the bottom of a large, heavy pot with vegetable oil. Salt and pepper the meat and brown it in the heated oil in batches to avoid crowding the pot and steaming the meat. Remove the meat to a plate as each piece is browned.

2. In the same fat, sauté the onions until soft. Replace the meat, cover the pot, and cook for about 1 hour over very low heat.

3. Pour the boiling water over the apricots and let soak for 30 minutes.

4. Preheat the oven to 300 °F.

5. After the meat has cooked for an hour, add the prunes and apricots and their soaking liquid to the pot, along with the carrots, sweet potatoes, lemon juice and peel, ginger, and cinnamon. Replace the cover and cook the tzimmes for another 2½ to 3 hours in the oven. During the last 30 to 45 minutes, remove the cover so the top browns. The tzimmes can be served immediately or reheated. It improves as it stands. It will keep in the refrigerator for at least a week and frozen for several months.
Serves 10

MEGINA

Matzo Meat Pie

Sephardim, particularly those from Turkey and Greece, make a layered matzo and meat pie. This one, from Rhodes, might be served at a Seder or as a main course during the week of Passover.

¼ cup vegetable oil
2 cups chopped onions
2 pounds ground beef or veal
1 cup minced dill and parsley
Salt
Freshly ground black pepper
6 eggs
5 matzos

1. Preheat the oven to 375°F. With a little of the oil, grease a 13-inch gratin dish or other baking dish with a capacity of about 3½ quarts.

2. Heat the remaining oil in a skillet and sauté the onions until they soften. Add the meat and, stirring, sauté until it is browned and all the clumps have broken up. Remove from the heat and pour off some of the accumulated fat. Add the herbs and taste for salt and pepper.

3. Beat 2 of the eggs just to combine the yolks and whites and add them to the meat.

4. In a pie plate or the skillet in which you cooked the meat, soak the whole matzos briefly in warm water, just until they soften and before they fall apart. Drain on paper towels.

5. Beat the remaining eggs just to combine. Place in the wiped-dry pie plate. Carefully dip 2 softened matzos into the eggs. Line the prepared pan with them, breaking the matzos into pieces to fit. Evenly spread the meat mixture over the matzos.

6. Soak the remaining matzos in the eggs and cover the meat with them. Pour any remaining eggs over the matzos.

7. Bake for 30 to 45 minutes, or until a rich brown crust forms. Cut into wedges and serve hot.

Serves 6 to 8

ROAST POULTRY

Roast capon, turkey, and chicken (if the crowd is small enough) are popular for Seder because they are easy to prepare and don't have to be served steaming hot, should the Seder go on longer than expected.

Thaw frozen birds in the refrigerator, allowing about 4 hours thawing time for each pound of poultry. A faster method is to put the well-wrapped bird in a basin or sink of cold water, allowing about 30 minutes of thawing time per pound. Before cooking, make sure you wash the bird, inside and out, and pat it dry. Also important: Wash the utensils, surfaces, and your hands with warm, soapy water after they have come in contact with raw poultry.

To roast an unstuffed bird, put quartered onions, quartered lemons, and a few sprigs of parsley in the cavity. Tie the legs together and twist the wing tips under the back. To roast a stuffed bird, do not stuff until you are ready to put the fowl in the oven. Place some stuffing in the neck cavity and cover it with the flap of neck skin; secure with a skewer. Spoon the stuffing into the body cavity, but don't pack it tightly. Tie the legs together and twist the wing tips, as for an unstuffed bird. Rub the poultry with a little vegetable oil and season with salt and pepper.

Roast on a rack, breast down, in an uncovered roasting pan, basting occasionally with pan juices. It is not necessary to turn the bird. For a turkey or capon, an instant meat thermometer inserted in the inside of the thigh between the leg and the body, but not touching the bone, should register 180°F; the breast should register 170°F and the stuffing 160°F. To test without a thermometer, move the leg joint up and down. It should give readily. Pierce the thigh; if the juices run clear, the bird is done. The problem with roasting poultry is that the breast cooks faster than the legs; when the breast meat is perfectly cooked the thigh joint will still be pink. If you object to bloody joints, resign yourself to somewhat overcooked breast meat. Follow the chart below for roasting times, and see pages 77-78 for recommended stuffings.

Allow ¾ to 1 pound of poultry per serving and roughly 15 minutes per pound for roasting. A stuffed bird will take longer to roast than will an unstuffed bird, and the larger the bird, the greater the time difference between cooking it stuffed or unstuffed. A 10-pound unstuffed turkey will cook in about 3½ hours; a stuffed 10-pound bird will take 4 hours. An unstuffed 25-pound turkey should be done in 5¼ hours; a stuffed one will take 6½ hours. Add 30 to 60 minutes onto the total time for a stuffed bird.

Bird	Weight	Oven Temp	Time
Capon	5 to 7 lb	325°F	2 hours
Chicken	2 to 3 lb	375°F	1 hour
	3½ to 4 lb	375°F	1¼ to 1¾ hours
	4½ to 5 lb	375°F	1½ to 2 hours
Turkey	6 to 8 lb	325°F	2½ to 3 hours
	8 to 14 lb	325°F	3¼ to 4¼ hours
	14 to 20 lb	325°F	4 to 4¾ hours
	20 to 25 lb	325°F	4¾ to 5¼ hours

TAGINE OF CHICKEN

This version of the famous Moroccan dish is often eaten by Sephardim at Passover. It's not difficult to prepare and it tastes superb. Perhaps best of all, it will wait.

One 3½- to 4-pound chicken, cut into
    serving pieces
½ cup matzo meal
6 tablespoons vegetable oil
2 cups chopped onions
1 cup chicken stock or water
1 teaspoon ground cinnamon
1 tablespoon grated fresh ginger
2 tablespoons lemon juice
1½ cups pitted prunes
2 tablespoons grated lemon peel
½ cup toasted slivered almonds

1. Wash and dry the chicken; set aside. Spread the matzo meal on a dinner plate. Dip the chicken pieces in the matzo meal to coat them lightly. Shake off the excess.

2. Heat the oil in a large sauté pan with a tight-fitting lid. Sauté the chicken pieces, in batches, on all sides until brown. Remove each piece to a platter as it is done.

3. Sauté the onions in the fat in the pan for about 15 minutes, or until soft, stirring with a wooden spoon to dislodge the brown bits on the bottom of the pan.

4. Combine the stock or water with the cinnamon, ginger, and lemon juice. Add the stock mixture to the sauté pan along with the browned chicken pieces. Cover and simmer gently for 20 minutes. Add the prunes and lemon peel and simmer for another 20 to 25 minutes, or until the chicken is tender. Check from time to time to make sure there is liquid in the pan; add water if necessary.

5. Place the chicken on a platter. Stir most of the almonds into the sauce and pour the sauce over the chicken. Sprinkle the remaining almonds on top. Serve immediately, or keep warm in a 200°F oven.

Serves 4

MINA DE PESAH

Matzo Chicken Pie

A Sephardic layered savory pie, this delicious dish seems designed for the turkey or chicken or capon leftover from the Seder or the chicken soup.

6 to 7 tablespoons vegetable oil
2 cups chopped onions
2 tablespoons minced garlic
1½ cups thinly sliced cultivated mushrooms
    (about ⅓ pound)
3 cups bite-sized pieces cooked chicken
    (about 14 ounces)
Salt
Freshly ground black pepper
1 cup chopped parsley
5 eggs, lightly beaten
5 to 6 matzos
1 cup chicken stock

1. Heat 5 tablespoons of the oil in a large skillet. Slowly sauté the onion and garlic until softened and translucent, about 10 minutes. Add the mushrooms and sauté until soft, an additional 5 minutes. Let cool. Stir in the chicken, salt, pepper, parsley, and eggs.

2. Preheat the oven to 375°F. Lightly oil a shallow 6-to 8-cup baking dish.

3. Dip 2 of the matzos into the stock until well moistened but not falling apart. Lay them in the baking dish, breaking pieces to fit. Spoon half the chicken mixture on top, and cover with 1 more moistened matzo, the remaining chicken, and the 2 remaining matzos. Pour 2 teaspoons oil over the top and bake for 15 minutes. Sprinkle with the remaining oil and bake an additional 15 minutes, or until the top is a rich, crisp brown. Let cool for 10 minutes, then serve.

Serves 6 to 8

HOT BORSCHT WITH MEAT

This is a splendid lunch or supper dish. Once the *rossl* is made, the borscht is a snap.

4 cups *rossl* liquid (see page 31)
3 cups diced *rossl* beets
4 cups water
2 onions, coarsely chopped
4 pounds flanken (short ribs) or brisket
5 eggs in the shell
1 tablespoon salt
Freshly ground black pepper
Lemon juice
Sugar
8 to 10 small potatoes, boiled and still warm

1. Combine the *rossl* liquid and beets with the water, onions, and meat in a large soup pot; carefully bury the eggs in the liquid. Bring to a boil, reduce the heat, and simmer, partially covered, for 2 to 3 hours, or until the meat is tender. Skim the foam as it rises.

2. Taste the borscht for seasoning; add salt, pepper, lemon juice if you like, and sugar, which it surely will require.

3. Serve the soup in individual bowls with a hot potato and all or part of a hard-boiled egg, which will have taken on a marbleized aspect from having cooked in the red liquid. Serve the meat as a second course or slice it and serve it in the soup.

If you have time, separate the vegetables and meat from the liquid. Refrigerate the liquid so you can easily remove the fat, which will harden on the top. Reheat to serve.

Serves 8 to 10

YOGURT-POTATO PIE

This slightly tart pie-pudding is a good lunch entree. Serve it with a green salad, steamed asparagus, or artichokes.

3½ to 4 cups chopped onions
4 tablespoons butter
1½ pounds potatoes, just boiled and
    still warm
Salt
Freshly ground black pepper
3 tablespoons potato starch
3 eggs, lightly beaten
2 cups plain yogurt (regular, low-fat, or non-fat)
¼ cup minced parsley

1. Preheat the oven to 350°F. Lightly grease a 10-inch pie plate.

2. Sauté the onions in the butter until softened and sweet, about 20 minutes.

3. While the onions cook, mash the still-warm potatoes with an old-fashioned potato masher or a fork, or put them through a food mill. Add the potatoes to the onions, combining well. Taste for salt and pepper.

4. Add the potato starch, stirring well to incorporate it completely. Add the eggs, yogurt, and parsley.

5. Turn the mixture into the prepared pan and bake for 40 minutes, or until the top is lightly browned. Serve hot or at room temperature.

Serves 6

VEGETABLE CUTLETS

This recipe, by Norma Schaffer of New Jersey, won a contest run by WOR Radio in New York. Its flavor and crunch make it the best of its type that I've ever tried.

1½ to 2 cups minced red or yellow peppers or
    a mixture of both
2 tablespoons olive oil
1½ cups grated carrots (4 carrots)
½ pound raw spinach, cleaned, trimmed of
    coarse stems, and chopped (2 tightly
      packed cups)
1 pound (3 medium) potatoes, boiled and
    mashed (2 cups)
6 tablespoons grated raw onion (1 large)
3 eggs, lightly beaten
1½ teaspoons salt
Freshly ground black pepper
1 cup matzo meal
Vegetable oil

1. Sauté the peppers in the olive oil until soft, about 15 or 20 minutes.

2. Add all of the remaining ingredients except the vegetable oil and let the mixture stand for 30 minutes or overnight, refrigerated. Bring to room temperature before continuing.

3. You can either fry or bake the cutlets. To fry them, heat about ¼ inch of vegetable oil in a large skillet. Form each patty with about ¼ cup of the mixture. Flatten the patties slightly and fry them in batches for about 6 minutes on the first side, then turn and fry for 3 or 4 minutes on the second side. Drain on paper towels and serve immediately.

To bake the cutlets, put the patties on a lightly greased baking sheet and place in a preheated 350°F oven for about 10 minutes; turn the patties and bake for another 7 to 10 minutes.

Makes about 40 patties; serves 6 to 8

SPINACH PIE

This Sephardic Passover spinach pie is good for a light lunch or as an accompaniment to a roast.

6 tablespoons olive or vegetable oil
2 pounds fresh spinach, or 2 packages thawed frozen spinach
2 cups chopped scallions, including some green tops (about 12)
1 cup matzo meal
1 cup chopped fresh dill
8 eggs
4 tablespoons lemon juice
2 whole matzos

1. Preheat the oven to 350°F. With 1 tablespoon of the oil, grease the bottom and sides of a shallow 2-quart baking dish. Set aside.

2. Clean the fresh spinach, if using, removing the thick stems; chop coarsely (you will have about 8 cups).

3. Heat the remaining 5 tablespoons of the oil in a heavy skillet. Add the scallions and, after a couple of minutes, the spinach. Stir until wilted and well combined with the oil. Stir in the matzo meal and combine well, using a wooden spoon. Add the dill. Remove the pan from the heat.

4. Beat the eggs with the lemon juice until frothy, 4 or 5 minutes in an electric mixer. Add the spinach, salt, and pepper.

5. Break the whole matzos and scatter the pieces on the bottom of the oiled pan. Pour the spinach mixture into the pan. Bake for 30 to 45 minutes, or until the top is nicely browned. Serve warm.

Serves 6 to 8

MATZO BREI

For a dish that has only two basic ingredients—matzos and eggs—*matzo brei* has a surprising number of variations. And people are passionate about their own. The first variant is the proportion of egg to matzo; the second is the style of cooking: pancake style, soufflé style, or scrambled-egg style. The third variant is the texture of the matzo: Should it remain crisp or should it be soggy? This last is a function of the preliminary soaking: Some people merely pass the matzo under cold water; others soak it in boiling water for 3 or 4 minutes. Try them all; then decide which you like best.

3 matzos
4 eggs
Salt
3 tablespoons butter
Sour cream
Jam, sugar, cinnamon

1. Break the matzos in half and then in half again. Soak them in hot water for 1 to 2 minutes. Remove and, with your hands, squeeze out as much water as you can.

2. Beat the eggs lightly with salt in a mixing bowl. Add the matzos and mix.

3. Heat the butter in a heavy skillet and, when it starts to turn brown, add the eggs and matzos. Either leave the mixture to set on the bottom and then turn as you would a pancake, or stir the mixture with a wooden spoon as you would scrambled eggs. By either method, the *matzo brei* will be done within 5 minutes, depending on how well done you like your eggs. Serve immediately with jam and/or sour cream, sugar or cinnamon.

To make the soufflé type of *matzo brei*, separate the eggs. Beat the yolks until they are thick and pale in color. Add the matzos to the yolks. Beat the whites until stiff and gently fold them into the yolk-matzo mixture. Cook in the butter as for the pancake variation.

Serves 2

MATZO MEAL PANCAKES

These are a delicious brunch or lunch dish: sweet and satisfying.

½ cup matzo meal
¾ teaspoon salt
1 tablespoon sugar
3 eggs, separated
½ cup cold water or milk or a combination
   of the two
Butter or vegetable oil for frying
Jam, warm honey (see Note), or sour cream

1. Combine the matzo meal, salt, and sugar.

2. Beat the egg yolks lightly, add the water and/or milk, and combine with the matzo-meal mixture.

3. Beat the egg whites until stiff but not dry. Fold into the matzo-meal batter.

4. Heat a film of butter or oil in a large, heavy skillet. Add the batter by tablespoonfuls. Fry for 3 or 4 minutes, turn the pancakes, and fry for another 2 or 3 minutes. The pancakes should be golden on both sides. Don't crowd the pan—a 10-inch skillet will hold 6 or 7 pancakes comfortably. Adjust the heat so neither the pancakes nor the fat burns, and add more butter or oil as necessary. Drain for a moment on paper towels and serve immediately with jam, warm honey, or sour cream.

Makes about 3 dozen 2-inch pancakes; serves 6

Variation: Add 1 cup chopped apple to the batter. To serve, sprinkle with 2 tablespoons sugar combined with 1 tablespoon ground cinnamon, or any of the suggested toppings for the plain pancakes.

Note: To warm honey, put the jar in a heatproof glass measuring cup filled with hot water; refill with hot water periodically.

VEGETABLES, KUGELS, AND STUFFINGS

Vegetables are not restricted at Passover, though grains certainly are. Some vegetables are traditionally served at the holiday because they are seasonal; others are served because they are easy. The vegetable selection here is small because so many of the vegetables you normally eat are permissible—no special recipes are necessary.

¶ Kugels (Yiddish for "puddings") are, in a word, delicious. Who can resist a potato kugel, with perhaps freshly made gribenes folded in? Or a matzo and cheese kugel? Though kugels are usually made of starch (the most famous is lokshen kugel, or noodle pudding), the apple and carrot kugel is mighty good, too.

ANJINARAS

Turkish Sweet and Sour Artichokes

Spring marks the first appearance of artichokes, and so, like asparagus, they are often served at Passover. This a refreshing salad to serve during the holiday.

8 fresh artichokes, or two 9-ounce packages frozen artichokes
¼ cup lemon juice (if using fresh artichokes, save the lemon shells)
2 tablespoons honey
2 tablespoons vegetable oil
¼ cup minced shallots
¼ cup chopped parsley

1. Slice off the woody stems of the fresh artichokes. Tug off the tough outer leaves. Turn each artichoke on its side and slice off about 1 inch from the top, exposing the pale interior. Snip off the spiny points of the remaining leaves. Quarter each artichoke and remove the hairy choke from the center. A scraping motion with a sharp paring knife works best. Add the quarters to the bowl of water in which you have placed the lemon shells, if you have them.

2. In a large pot, bring a quart of water to a boil with the honey, lemon juice, and oil. Add the artichokes, lower the heat, and cook, covered, for 40 to 45 minutes for fresh artichokes, or until tender but not mushy. Frozen artichokes, which need not be defrosted, will cook in 6 to 8 minutes.

3. With a slotted spoon, transfer the artichokes to a serving bowl. Combine with the shallots. Boil down the cooking liquid until it is syrupy and reduced in volume to about ½ cup. Pour this liquid over the artichokes. Let cool to room temperature and serve sprinkled with the parsley. The artichokes will keep, covered, in the refrigerator, for several days.

Serves 6 to 8

ASPARAGUS

Asparagus is the very definition of spring and the most seasonally appropriate as well as delicious vegetable to serve at Passover. They can be served either hot or at room temperature, and all the preparation can be done in advance.

Asparagus (all as close to the same size as possible)
Melted butter or margarine
Lemon wedges
Chopped parsley
Lemon juice
Olive oil
Hard-boiled eggs

1. If the asparagus stalks are thin, merely break off the woody bottom of each one. If thick, cut off the bottom and pare each one to the pale green part of the stalk, all the way to the tip.

2. Put the asparagus in a large skillet of boiling water, making sure the skillet is large enough to hold the stalks without bending them; a 10-inch skillet is usually large enough. Add salt and cook the asparagus until tender but not mushy, anywhere from 5 to 15 minutes, depending on the diameter of the stalks. Remove with a slotted spoon to several layers of paper towels.

3. If you are serving the asparagus hot, accompany them with melted butter or margarine, lemon wedges, and parsley. If serving at room temperature, leave them on the paper towels until just before serving. Make a dressing of 1 part lemon juice to 3 parts olive oil and garnish by pressing the hard-boiled eggs through a sieve. If you've had enough eggs, just sprinkle with parsley.

The asparagus shouldn't be dressed much more than 30 minutes before serving.

1 pound of asparagus makes 2 to 3 servings

HONEYED CARROTS

1 pound carrots (about 8), sliced
3 tablespoons orange juice or water
1 teaspoon grated lemon peel
3 tablespoons butter or margarine
1 teaspoon salt
1 teaspoon grated fresh ginger
3 tablespoons honey
¼ cup chopped dill

1. Combine the carrots, orange juice, lemon peel, butter or margarine, salt, ginger, and honey in a saucepan. Place over low heat, cover, and cook for about 20 minutes, or until the carrots are tender.

2. Sprinkle with dill and serve.

Serves 4

CARROT AND APPLE KUGEL

This is a light and fresh-tasting *kugel*.

¼ cup vegetable oil or melted margarine
1 pound (about 8) carrots
1 pound (about 3) apples
1 teaspoon sugar
⅓ cup matzo meal
½ teaspoon ground nutmeg
½ teaspoon lemon juice
½ teaspoon grated lemon peel
¾ cup toasted slivered almonds

1. Preheat the oven to 350°F. Lightly oil a 4-cup pie plate or gratin dish.

2. Scrape the carrots and grate them in a food processor or a standing electric mixer with a fine grater attachment, or by hand with a box grater; you should have about 4 cups.

3. Peel and core the apples and grate them; you should have about 1 cup.

4. Combine all the ingredients except ¼ cup of the toasted almonds in a bowl and mix well. Coarsely grate or process the remaining ¼ cup toasted almonds.

5. Transfer the contents of the bowl to the prepared baking dish, sprinkle with the grated almonds, and place in the oven for 20 to 30 minutes, or until the mixture is heated through and a few brown spots appear on the top. Serve hot or warm.

Serves 6 to 8

SAUTÉED CELERY

Celery is a versatile vegetable that isn't often enough served cooked. Here's a quick, easy, and tasty side dish, good for Passover and other times of the year as well.

1 head celery (about 16 stalks)
3 tablespoons olive oil
1 tablespoon minced garlic
1½ cups drained, chopped tomatoes (fresh or canned)
¼ cup minced parsley

1. Discard the celery leaves; string the stalks and chop them into ½- to 1-inch segments. Steam the celery for about 6 or 7 minutes, or until it is barely tender.

2. Heat the oil in a skillet and slowly sauté the garlic for 2 or 3 minutes; don't let it brown. Add the tomato and celery to the skillet and sauté, stirring occasionally, for about 15 minutes. The celery should be tender but not limp. Sprinkle with parsley and serve. If you plan to reheat this dish, undercook the celery slightly.

Serves 6 to 8

POTATO CHREMSEL

Light and delicate, these puffs are a good accompaniment to broiled fish or a simple roast.

1½ pounds all-purpose or baking potatoes
3 eggs, separated
2 tablespoons salt
Freshly ground black pepper
1 to 1½ cups vegetable oil for frying

1. Cover the unpeeled potatoes with cold water, bring to a boil, and cook until they are tender.

2. As soon as the potatoes are cool enough to handle, peel them. Put them through a food mill or potato ricer; don't use a food processor for this step because it will create gummy potatoes.

3. Beat the egg yolks into the potatoes, one at a time, beating to incorporate each one before you add the next. Season with salt and pepper.

4. Beat the egg whites until they hold their shape firmly, but aren't dry. Stir half of them into the potatoes and fold in the remaining half.

5. Heat ¼ inch of oil in a large heavy skillet. (A 10-inch skillet will take 1¼ cups.) Drop the potatoes in by tablespoonfuls. Don't crowd the pan; a 10-inch skillet will hold 7 or 8 *chremsel* at once. Fry the *chremsel* on each side until golden. Remove to paper towels to drain. Add more oil as necessary and regulate the heat so the next batch of puffs doesn't burn. Serve as soon as you have a plateful to pass. The poor cook keeps frying until all the batter is used—folks never seem to say, "Stop. We've had enough."

Makes about 35 1½-inch puffs; serves 8 to 10.

VEGETABLE TZIMMES

Tzimmes, a dish of spiced and sweetened vegetables, fruit, and meat (see page 43 for a tzimmes with meat), is versatile and almost infinitely variable. Because of the variety of ingredients that must be scrubbed, peeled, sliced, diced, and simmered, the Yiddish word *tzimmes* is synonymous with a complicated chore or unnecessary fuss. This tzimmes isn't *that* arduous, and it's really delicious.

2 pounds (about 12 large) carrots, peeled and cut into 1-inch slices
2 pounds sweet potatoes, peeled and cut into 1-inch dice
1 pound white potatoes, peeled and cut into 1-inch dice
1 cup chopped prunes
¼ cup honey
¼ teaspoon ground cinnamon
¼ teaspoon grated nutmeg
2 teaspoons grated lemon peel
1 tablespoon butter or margarine

1. Preheat the oven to 350°F.

2. Cook the carrots in boiling water for cover for 5 minutes. Add the sweet potatoes and white potatoes and cook 5 minutes more. The vegetables should be barely tender. Drain.

3. Combine the carrots and sweet and white potatoes with the prunes, honey, cinnamon, nutmeg, lemon peel, and 1 cup of water. Turn the mixture into a shallow 3-quart baking dish. Dot the top with butter or margarine and bake for 30 minutes. If the top becomes too brown, cover it with aluminum foil.

Serves 8 to 10

POTATO KUGEL

This simple *kugel* can be made in advance, but don't stop working until it's in the pan, ready to be baked.

2½ pounds potatoes, well scrubbed
10 to 15 garlic cloves
2 tablespoons schmaltz, melted and cooled
2 to 3 tablespoons chicken soup
Gribenes **(see Schmaltz, page 21), optional**
Salt
Freshly ground black pepper

1. Steam the potatoes and garlic until the potatoes are soft. This will take anywhere from 15 to 60 minutes, depending on their size.

2. Preheat the oven to 350°F. Lightly grease a shallow 4-cup baking pan.

3. While they are still hot, mash the potatoes and the garlic with an old-fashioned potato masher or pass them through a food mill. Leave the skin on for added color and texture.

4. Combine the potatoes with the schmaltz, chicken soup, and the optional *gribenes*. Taste for salt and pepper. Place the mixture in the prepared pan and bake for 20 to 30 minutes, or until the top is nicely browned.

Serves 6 to 8

MATZO AND CHEESE KUGEL

Think of this as a blintze loaf for Passover. It is good as part of a dairy supper or as a light meal on its own.

5 eggs
1 cup milk
1 pound cottage cheese
1 teaspoon salt
¼ cup honey
½ teaspoon ground cinnamon
4 matzos, broken into pieces
½ cup toasted slivered almonds

1. Preheat the oven to 350°F. Lightly grease a shallow 2-quart baking dish or large pie plate.

2. Beat together the eggs and milk. Add the cottage cheese, salt, honey, and cinnamon.

3. Place half the matzo pieces in the baking dish. Pour half the cheese-egg mixture on top. Sprinkle with the almonds. Cover with the remaining matzo pieces and the rest of the cheese-egg mixture. Bake for about 40 minutes, or until the top is brown and slightly crunchy.

Serves 6 to 10

MATZO FARFEL KUGEL

Matzo farfel looks like egg noodle dough *(chometz!)*, but is made from matzo. This is a traditional *kugel* and a good one, too.

1½ cups diced onions
2 tablespoons schmaltz
2 cups matzo farfel
4 eggs
Salt
Freshly ground black pepper
Gribenes **(see Schmaltz, page 21), optional**

1. Preheat the oven to 350F. Lightly grease a shallow 6-cup ovenproof pan.

2. Cook the onions in the schmaltz until softened, about 10 minutes.

3. Cover the farfel with 2 cups boiling water. Drain after 5 minutes, pressing out as much liquid as possible.

4. In a large bowl, lightly beat the eggs just to combine the yolks and whites. Add the onions, farfel, salt, and pepper. If you have any *gribenes,* add them. Mix well.

5. Transfer the *kugel* to the prepared pan and bake for about 30 minutes, or until it is brown on top and set. Serve immediately.

Serves 6

MATZO FARFEL AND APPLE KUGEL

This is the perfect accompaniment to a simple roast chicken or brisket; it's also good with broiled or sautéed fish, in which case you might want to substitute butter for the vegetable oil or margarine.

5 tablespoons vegetable oil or melted and cooled margarine
2 cups matzo farfel
4 eggs
1 teaspoon salt
1 teaspoon sugar
½ cup water
2 apples, peeled, cored, and sliced
1 teaspoon lemon juice
½ teaspoon grated lemon peel
¼ cup ground walnuts

1. Preheat the oven to 350°F. With some of the oil or margarine, lightly grease a 1-quart baking dish.

2. Combine the farfel with 2 of the eggs. Place the mixture in a heavy skillet over low heat and toast the farfel. Stir constantly until the farfel is golden and the pieces are separate.

3. Beat the remaining 2 eggs with the salt, sugar, and 3 tablespoons of the vegetable oil or margarine. Add the farfel and ½ cup of water.

4. Line the bottom of the prepared dish with half of the apple slices and sprinkle them with the lemon juice and lemon peel. Add the farfel and the remaining apple slices. Pour over the remaining oil or margarine, and sprinkle with nuts. Bake for 25 to 35 minutes.

Serves 6 to 8

MATZO FRUIT STUFFING

2 cups chopped onions
4 tablespoons schmaltz or vegetable oil
10 matzos, crumbled
1 cup chopped stewed prunes
1 egg, lightly beaten
1 cup diced tart apple
½ cup raisins
1 teaspoon grated lemon peel
2 cups chicken soup or water

1. In a large skillet, sauté the onions slowly in the schmaltz or oil until they are soft and starting to color, about 15 minutes.

2. Add the crumbled matzos and sauté slowly for 10 more minutes. Transfer to a large bowl and add the remaining ingredients. Set aside until ready to stuff the bird. Any leftover stuffing should be baked, covered, in a casserole. The timing will depend on the depth of the pan.

Makes about 4 cups, enough for a 10- to 12-pound bird

MUSHROOM STUFFING

This delicious, moist stuffing can be made several hours in advance of stuffing the bird. Keep the stuffing in a cool place.

4 cups chopped onions
¼ cup schmaltz or vegetable oil
1 pound cultivated mushrooms, thinly sliced
   (4½ cups)
1 teaspoon salt
2 eggs
½ cup matzo meal
½ cup chopped parsley

1. Sauté the onions slowly in the schmaltz or oil for 15 to 20 minutes, or until soft and translucent.

2. Add the mushrooms and cook for about 10 more minutes, or until they are tender. Taste for salt.

3. Beat the eggs just to combine the yolks and whites. Add the matzo meal and parsley. Combine this mixture with the onion-mushroom mixture and use it to stuff the bird.

Makes about 4 cups stuffing, enough for a 10- to 12-pound bird

DESSERTS

Passover is a time for creative bakers to shine: no flour, no cornstarch, no baking soda or baking powder—it's a real challenge to serve a cake or cookies worth eating. This chapter includes several tried-and-true, easy, almost-no-fail cake recipes.
¶ After the Seder, a long and heavy meal, fruit salad and macaroons are a good choice. During the rest of the week, cakes are welcome. If you can't resist showing off at the Seder, make the banana cake—it's very tasty and it keeps well; inevitably, there will be leftovers.

DRIED FRUIT COMPOTE

This is a staple of the Passover kitchen: It keeps well and tastes good; it's delicious for dessert, a snack, or at lunch with yogurt or cottage cheese.

**4 pounds mixed dried fruit (prunes, apricots,
  apples, pears, figs)**
1½ cups orange juice
1½ cups water
½ cup sugar
One 5-inch cinnamon stick
**Peel of 1 lemon, removed in 1 or more
  large pieces**

1. To remove the sulfates used as a preservative in packaged dried fruit, pour boiling water over the the fruit and let stand for at least 1 hour. Drain thoroughly.

2. Put the fruit in a saucepan with all of the remaining ingredients. Bring to a boil, lower the heat, and simmer gently for 30 to 45 minutes, or until the fruit is tender.

3. Let the fruit cool in the saucepan. Taste to determine if more sugar or lemon or orange juice is needed. Store the fruit in any syrup that remains (the fruit will absorb most of the liquid) covered in the refrigerator. Remove the cinnamon stick.

The compote will keep, refrigerated, until Shavouth easily and will probably still be good at Succot.

Serves 10 to 12

Variation: Drain the fruit of any liquid and place in a shallow ovenproof pan such as a pie plate, gratin dish, or casserole. Barely cover the fruit with some of its syrup; sprinkle the top with crumbled macaroons, and bake for 15 to 20 minutes in a preheated 350°F oven. Serve warm or at room temperature.

COCONUT MACAROONS

Vegetable oil
3 egg whites
½ cup sugar
2 teaspoons lemon juice
1 tablespoon grated lemon peel
2 cups (6 ounces) finely grated unsweetened
  coconut

1. Preheat the oven to 275°F. Line 2 cookie sheets with wax paper and grease the paper lightly with vegetable oil.

2. Beat the egg whites until foamy. Gradually add the sugar and beat until the eggs are stiff and shiny. Add the lemon juice and peel. Gently fold the coconut into the whites, mixing just to combine.

3. Put the batter in a pastry bag fitted with a 7B or 8 star tip and pipe cookies onto the cookie sheets. Alternatively, form the macaroons with 2 teaspoons and place on the sheet. Bake for 45 to 60 minutes, or until the macaroons are lightly colored. Halfway through the baking, switch the cookie sheets, top to bottom, front to back. Let the macaroons cool on a wire rack before storing them in an airtight container, where they'll keep for several days. These cookies also may be frozen.

Makes about 40 macaroons

ALMOND MACAROONS

Macaroons are a Passover classic. They are usually store-bought, packed in a vacuum can. These are better. Try them.

Vegetable oil
4 egg whites, at room temperature
½ teaspoon almond extract
½ cup sugar
Scant 2 cups (½ pound) finely ground blanched almonds
1½ tablespoons toasted slivered almonds

1. Preheat the oven to 300°F. Line 2 cookie sheets with wax paper and lightly grease the paper with vegetable oil.

2. Beat the egg whites until stiff but not dry; add the almond extract to the almost-stiff whites.

3. Combine the sugar and ground almonds. Stir about one fourth of the whites into the almond mixture and then gently fold in the remaining whites.

4. Place the mixture in a pastry bag fitted with a 7B star tube and pipe out onto the cookie sheets, or form the macaroons with 2 teaspoons. Place a toasted slivered almond on top of each macaroon. Bake for 30 to 40 minutes, or until the tops are lightly browned. Halfway through the baking, switch the cookie sheets, top to bottom and front to back. Cool the macaroons on wire racks before storing them in an airtight container, where they'll keep for several days. They also freeze well.

Makes about 40 macaroons

CHOCOLATE NUT CAKE

The first time I made this cake I forgot to add the matzo meal—the cake was moist and delicious. I don't recommend your leaving out the matzo meal, but I do want to reassure you that the recipe is forgiving.

6 eggs, separated
1½ cups sugar
1½ cups chopped walnuts
2 ounces semisweet chocolate, grated (see Note)
2 ounces unsweetened chocolate, grated (see Note)
2 Delicious apples, grated
½ cup matzo meal

1. Preheat the oven to 350 °F. Lightly grease a 9-inch springform pan or line it, bottom and sides, with baking parchment.

2. Beat the egg yolks until thick. Add the sugar and beat briefly. Add all the remaining ingredients except the egg whites.

3. Beat the egg whites until stiff but not dry. Stir about one fourth of the whites into the yolk mixture; carefully fold in the rest.

4. Pour the batter into the prepared springform pan and bake for 35 to 45 minutes, or until the cake pulls away from the sides of the pan and a toothpick inserted in the center of the cake comes out clean. Let the cake cool in the pan before removing the sides. Well wrapped, the cake will keep for several days.

Serves 8

Note: The best way to grate chocolate is in a Mouli hand grater. The chocolate must be perfectly dry.

WALNUT CAKE

My friend Arthur Schwartz's mother, Sydelle, and her mother before her, made this cake year after year. And it remains a star in the modest firmament of Passover baking.

9 eggs, at room temperature, separated
1 cup sugar
2 cups walnuts, ground to a powder
** (see Note)**
2 tablespoons matzo cake meal
1 teaspoon pure vanilla extract
⅛ teaspoon salt

1. Preheat the oven to 350°F. Dust a 10-by-3½-inch loose-bottomed metal tube pan or two 9-by-3-inch loaf pans with a little extra cake meal and set aside.

2. With an electric mixer, beat the egg yolks until pale in color. Beat in the sugar 2 tablespoons at a time, beating well after each addition.

3. Combine the nuts with the matzo cake meal. Stir into the yolks along with the vanilla.

4. Beat the egg whites with the salt until they are stiff but not dry. Fold them gently and carefully into the batter.

5. Turn the batter into the prepared pan(s) and smooth the top. Bake for 30 to 40 minutes, or until the cake shrinks away from the side of the pan(s) and a cake tester inserted in the center of the cake(s) comes out clean. Let cool in the pan(s) on a rack.

6. To serve, run a knife around the edge of the tube pan and around the tube. Place the pan on a bottle and let the side slip off. Turn upside down on a cake plate. The cake should fall away from the tube and the bottom; if it doesn't, give it a tap or run the knife again around the tube and the bottom of the cake. If presentation is less important to you, leave the cake attached to the bottom and the tube—there's less risk of the cake's sinking. If using loaf pans, run a knife around the edge of the pans and invert the pans.

Makes one 10-inch tube cake or two 9-by-3-inch loaf cakes; serves 10

Note: The best way to grind the walnuts is in a hand-held Mouli grater, such as the ones sold for grating cheese or parsley. In a food processor the walnuts will turn greasy and clump, and you'll never achieve the fine powder you need for this cake.

BANANA NUT CAKE

This cake, well covered, will keep for several days.

Vegetable oil
1¼ cups ground toasted almonds
7 eggs, separated
1 cup sugar
1 tablespoon lemon juice
3 very ripe bananas, mashed (1½ cups)
½ teaspoon salt
1 teaspoon grated lemon peel
¾ cup potato starch

1. Preheat the oven to 350°F. Lightly grease a 10-by-3½-inch tube pan or 10-inch springform pan with vegetable oil and dust with a few tablespoons of ground almonds. Make sure all surfaces have a coating of oil and nuts, or the cake will be difficult to remove from the pan.

2. Using an electric mixer, beat the yolks until they are thick and pale in color, about 3 minutes. Add the sugar and lemon juice and beat for about 5 minutes, or until the mixture makes a continuous ribbon when the beaters are lifted.

3. Stir in the bananas, salt, lemon peel, and almonds. Sift in the potato starch. Beat for a minute or two.

4. Beat the egg whites until they hold soft peaks. Stir one fourth of them into the batter until no trace of white remains. Gently fold the remaining whites into the batter.

5. Pour the mixture into the prepared pan to within ½ inch of the top; smooth the top. Bake for 30 to 40 minutes, or until a skewer comes out clean and the top is nicely browned. Let the cake cool completely on a rack; it will sink as it cools. Run a thin knife around the edge and the tube of the tube pan and release the cake carefully. Or, run a thin knife around the edge of the springform pan, release the cake, and then remove the bottom of the pan.

Makes one 10-inch tube cake or round cake; serves 8 to 10

BIRMUELOS

Doughnuts

These Sephardic doughnuts can be served as a sweet or savory course. This sweet version is delicious for breakfast or dessert. Similar to the Askenazic matzo meal pancake (page 58), *birmuelos* are really good hot from the skillet without the coating, or warm, with the honey and nut layer. They don't keep, so be prepared to serve them immediately.

Syrup
1 cup water
½ cup honey
¼ cup sugar
3 tablespoons lemon juice

Doughnuts
6 matzos
Milk and/or water
4 eggs, lightly beaten
Salt

Vegetable oil for frying

Coating
1 cup toasted almonds, ground to a powder
½ teaspoon ground cinnamon
1 teaspoon sugar

1. Make the syrup first because it must chill before you can use it. Combine the water, honey, and sugar in a heavy saucepan. Bring to a boil and simmer, watching carefully as the liquid tends to boil over, until the mixture coats the back of a spoon, about 20 minutes. Add the lemon juice and remove from the heat. Let cool and chill.

2. To make the doughnuts: Break the matzos into sixths or eighths, or even smaller pieces, and cover with milk or a combination of milk and water. Let stand for at least 1 hour. Squeeze out the moisture and mash the matzos in a bowl with a wooden spoon until relatively smooth. Add the eggs and salt.

3. In a heavy skillet, heat about 1 inch of oil. By half-tablespoonfuls, add the *birmuelos* dough to the oil in batches. Don't flatten the pieces of dough to pancake size—leave them as irregular balls. Turn the *birmuelos* in the hot oil until they are brown all over. Remove with a slotted spoon to paper towels to drain. Don't crowd the pan, and continually adjust the heat so that the oil remains hot but not burning.

4. To make the coating: Combine the nuts, cinnamon, and sugar in a small bowl and spread on a plate.

5. Dip the warm *birmuelos* in the syrup and then roll them in the coating. Serve immediately.

Makes about 4 dozen doughnuts

INGBERLACH

Walnut Candy

This traditional Passover sweet is similar to the more familiar *nuant*.

1 egg
2 cups matzo farfel
1⅓ cups honey
½ cup sugar
½ cup lemon or orange juice
2 tablespoons grated fresh ginger
1 cup chopped walnuts

1. Preheat the oven to 250°F.

2. Beat the egg slightly and mix with the farfel; make sure all pieces are coated. Spread on a 14-by-18-inch cookie sheet and bake for about 30 minutes, or until the pieces of farfel are dry, separate, and shiny. Stir every 10 minutes or so to ensure even browning. When the farfel cools, you may need to separate some of the pieces with your fingers.

3. In a deep, heavy pan, combine the honey, sugar, lemon or orange juice, and ginger. Bring the mixture to a boil over medium heat, stirring until the sugar dissolves. Add the farfel and boil gently, stirring occasionally, until the mixture starts to thicken and turns light brown. Add the nuts and continue to cook about 15 minutes longer, or until the mixture is sticky, looks like caramel, and barely drops off a lifted spoon.

4. With wine, juice, or oil, wet the cookie sheet on which you toasted the farfel and pour the mixture onto it. Dampen a rolling pin or a wooden spoon with more wine or juice and pat the mixture out to form a relatively smooth layer about ¼ inch thick. Let cool completely. Cut diagonally into bite-sized pieces and remove with a flexible metal spatula to an airtight container. Alternatively, with moistened hands, form the candy into walnut-sized balls.

Makes 1½ pounds candy

INDEX

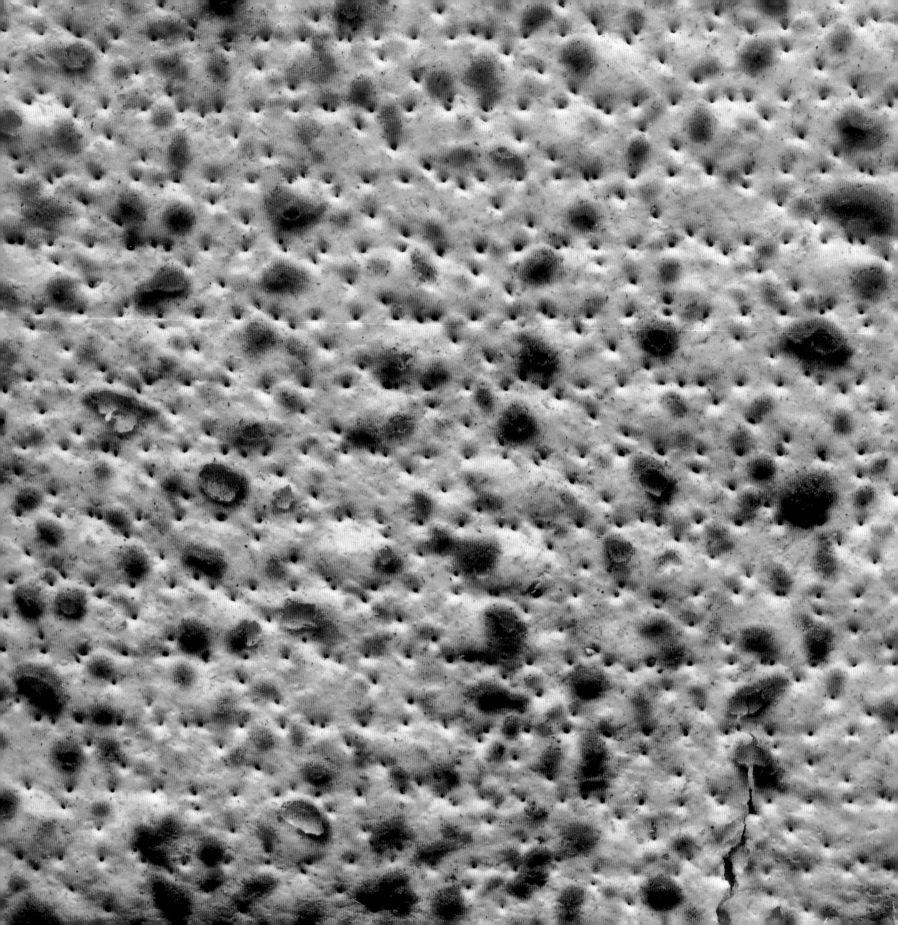